THE SESSION WITH HARIO
NOW IT'S YOUR TURN TO WIN

THE SESSION WITH HARIO
NOW IT'S YOUR TURN TO WIN

A Self-Help Book

Harry Thornton
aka "HarioOvadtop"

HarioOvadtop International Publishing
Fort Washington, Maryland

THE SESSION WITH HARIO
NOW IT'S YOUR TURN TO WIN

Published by:
HarioOvadtop International Publishing
Fort Washington, Maryland
harioovadtop@yahoo.com

Harry Thornton, Publisher / Editorial Director
Yvonne Rose/Quality Press.info, Book Packager

Paperback ISBN #: 979-8-218-96592-1

Library of Congress Control Number: 2023919594

Dedication

I would like to dedicate this book to my first-born child.
-Brittany Latisha Everett-
who is deceased, and to
my Father who taught me how to love
-Harry Freeman Thornton-
who is also deceased.

I would like to share encouraging words
from my father and my daughter
-Words from my father-
"Boy, you can do anything you want to do."
Words from my daughter-
from her Fantabulous Friday message
If you dream it, get up and go hard for it,
Appreciate the little things and stop comparing,
Stop complaining, be the change that you want to see.
Remain focused. As soon as you take your eyes off the prize
your demise is right around the corner.

Have an Awesomely Amazing day!

Acknowledgements

I wish to acknowledge and give special thanks to God
for getting me through this whole process.
Even though I was disobedient,
You never betrayed me.

Thank you for introducing Yourself to me
in a way that I can prove
You are here.

Special acknowledgements
to my mother DeLois Johnson and
my brother Keith "Keifdane" Thornton
for always being there for me, and to
my friend Tonry Allen who gave me solid advice
in times when I needed it the most.
I would also like to acknowledge the members of the
Huddle all over the world and my
Facebook Group
Narcissist Anonymous 101- the Empath Tribe.

Preface

This book is about the phases I created during my one-on-one coaching sessions to individuals around the world who are dealing with a person who has Narcissist Personality Disorder (NPD).

For the past three years, since 2020, I've spoken with thousands of individuals during my one-on-one sessions around the globe to include Africa, Asia, Australia, Brazil, Britain, China, Dubai, Europe, Holland, Italy, Mexico, Philippines, Spain, Russia, United Kingdom, Caribbean Islands, Hawaii and throughout the United States.

This book has been created to help you stop ruminating and to strengthen you from the inside out and it will also help you to bring closure from a narcissistic relationship. I included nine exercises to support you through your journey to heal from the pain that you experienced while in the narcissist relationship. This was a process I went through myself having dealt with narcissism for most of my adult life.

In 2019, I was inspired by other YouTubers who were speaking on the topic of narcissism and at that point, I decided to create my own YouTube channel- Harioovadtop. I made my first video titled *"Does the Narcissist Treat the New Supply Better"* on February 2, 2020 and I knew that helping people was the calling on my life.

This was the beginning of my new mission to help others that suffer in silence and do not know how to get out.

Contents

Introduction

Welcome to my office. My name is Harioovadtop you are obviously here because you want information that will give you a better understanding of what narcissism is all about and I'm giving you information that you will not get in a classroom. So, the first question I ask everyone is, "*Why do you think you are dealing with a narcissist?*"

The Google definition of a narcissist - a person who has an excessive interest in or admiration of themselves. My definition of a narcissist- is a person that has ill intent toward You/a Devil or Demon. Did the narcissist do this to you- *Did they abuse you? Did they gaslight you? Did they future fake you? Did they manipulate you? Did they use you? Did they cheat on you?*

To say you are dealing with a narcissist the person must have at least two or more of these traits.

NOTES

CHAPTER 1

The Decision

I want you to briefly give me some background on what you have gone through with the narcissist and then tell me what you believe makes this person a narcissist.

Tell me where you currently are with the narcissist meaning, are you currently with the person in a relationship? Did they discard you for a new supply or did the narcissist force you to discard them?

To get this process started in getting your life back to a place where you win,

You must first make a **Decision.**

What are you realistically willing to do to win?

Are you willing to do the work that it will take to get your life back?

Are you willing to make the sacrifices that it will take to get your life back?

Are you tired of being tired, are you sick of being sick, are you done with being done?

Let's get to it- first and foremost define the word decision. A decision is an action. It requires something getting done and the power of making a decision is life changing... the sooner you make the decision, the sooner your life starts changing for the better.

So, you ask yourself, what decision do I have to make? The decision that you have to make is, what is the most important thing in your life? Is it your happiness or is it everyone else's happiness?

If you chose your happiness, then continue to read this book because it will help change your life. For those who chose everyone else's happiness, give this book to someone who needs it because this book was written for people who want to be happy and are willing to do the work for a better life.

<u>EXERCISE #1</u>: The moment you wake up every day, you must decide that today I am going to have a great day and I am going to be happy. You must make a decision daily to be happy. Your life must come first. All of your life, you have put everyone else's happiness before your own and today it's time to put your happiness first. You must decide that it's your turn to be happy. You must be willing to do the work to be happy. You must envision yourself being happy. You must think that you are happy. You must become obsessed with your happiness. You have to rewire your chain of thought to be happy first every day.

Happiness comes to those who work towards it. Your happiness is now your new obsession. Your job, your business, your spouse, your children or anything else outside of you can manipulate your happiness.

It is important, NO, it is *vital* that you learn that true happiness comes from within, not from the outside.

NOTES

CHAPTER 2

No Contact

Your life and your actions have brought you to the place you're currently in. The same way you decided to purchase this book, you will have to make a decision about your future. At this point, you may think that you have decided on what you are going to do in the future, so let me ask you, "what actions have you put in place that will permanently change the future of your relationship with the narcissist?"

If you have decided that your happiness comes first, you must go **No Contact** with the narcissist. If any changes are going to happen in your life, you must be willing to take a big step; the next step in this process is No Contact. So, have you gone No Contact? Going No Contact is the single most important part of this process because it shows you have made a decision, it shows you have created a boundary, it shows you are now taking charge of your life again.

The narcissist should be blocked on social media and on your cell phone and your email if possible. The reason that the narcissist should be blocked from being able to call your phone is because, every time your phone rings, you know it's not the narc because they are blocked. The purpose of the block is so that your phone no longer triggers you to think about the narcissist, which forces you to ruminate about them. Your phone no longer triggers you when it rings because the narc is blocked, it no longer triggers you when you get a text message because the narc is blocked, it no longer triggers you when you get an email because the narc is blocked.

Without this action this process will not work. Please do not make yourself another person trying to prove this process wrong. Many have tried to stay in contact with the narcissist and that has led them to the place you are in now. They were all trying to get out and none were successful and if you stay in contact with the narcissist, you won't get out of this either.

<u>EXERCISE #2</u> Block all social media accounts connected with the narcissist- block telephone numbers, block email accounts. Assume the narcissist is following you on fake accounts, so you may have to block people that you don't know. Also be aware of the narcissist following your family members and friends because even if they can't follow you directly, they will follow people that they know you associate with just to try to see how they can keep up with you.

NOTES

____

____

____

____

____

____

____

____

____

____

CHAPTER 3

Rumination & Self-Betrayal

Rumination defined is a deep or considered thought about something also known as the constant obsessive thought about a person that you are no longer in a relationship with, and you don't have closure. After being discarded by or being forced to discard a narcissist, usually it ends without you having closure. One of the reasons that a narcissist doesn't give you closure is to force you to ruminate. The main reason that you think you are ruminating is because of the pain that you believe came from the betrayal of the narcissist you were dealing with. You are trying to figure out why the narcissist that you did everything for, would lie, cheat, steal, gaslight and manipulate you the way they did. As a matter of fact, the narcissist did things to you that you are completely ashamed of, and yet, you still feel remorse towards the narcissist the same way that someone would feel the

"Stockholm Syndrome" towards someone who has done something bad to them.

The reality of it all is that you are in the pain that you are in because not only did you stay with the narcissist after being lied to, after being cheated on, after all the manipulation, after being gaslit, after being future faked with. The betrayal that is worse than all of that combined, is that YOU not only stayed with that person, but you wanted to continue working on the relationship, which means you also betrayed YOU.

Self-betrayal is the most painful thing that you could do to yourself because it means that while you were being attacked by the narcissist, you actively participated in the attack that is against YOU. While going through this entire process, your inner voice has been telling you what to do and you have not been listening.

In this book I want to tell you exactly how I went from the worst hell to the happiest place in my life.

You dealt with a narcissist as many of us have and now either you are with this person living in hell or you have been discarded by the person, or you have been forced to discard them and you are trying to figure out, *why am I still in so much pain?*

What I have learned in my personal experience is through all the mental, physical, and financial abuse I endured, the narcissist had very little, if anything to do with all the pain that I suffered. The reality is that the narcissist was never the cause of my pain nor my issues. I thought that for sure this person was the reason at the end of this and I found out that she was not. Yes! This person was abusive in every way and in every form possible, disrespectful beyond anything you can imagine and now she was out of my life. *So why did I still think about her daily... because the problem was no longer in my life? Why did it hurt so bad? Why was I obsessively still ruminating about this person?*

Now I realized after thinking for hours, days, and months trying to figure out why I was still in pain for so long when the person who had been treating me so bad, lied, cheated, and stole was no longer in my life. So why was I still obsessively ruminating daily? I realized although this person had betrayed me in every way humanly possible, this dirty low-life cruttbawl betrayal was nothing in comparison to the way I betrayed myself. I never knew, until this point, that accepting the fact that I betrayed myself is far worse than any betrayal coming from her or anyone else, for that matter. At that point, I realized that the pain I felt was the pain of self-betrayal.

Self-betrayal feels like white noise. In my mind, I looked at all of the arguments and disrespect that I thought was me standing up for myself and having boundaries. I grew to realize that me responding and arguing, being involved on any level with someone that is disrespectful was in fact disrespecting myself. I say this because this was not the first time and it was not the 101st time either, there has been so much disrespect, I could not begin to count how many times I was disrespected. I grew accustomed to the disrespect, and I began to normalize it the same way I ate lunch every day...it was my new normal.

So, let's talk about self-betrayal and what that LOOKS like. Self-betrayal looks like "*I'm doing everything to save my family*"; "*I'm doing what I have to do to save my marriage*"; *I don't want to fail*"; "*I want to break the cycle of failed marriages in my family*"; " *I want to win*"- all of these are examples of how we make excuses to betray ourselves. I'm trying to make sense of something that doesn't make sense. I'm tired of being tired. I'm done with being done. I'm finished with being finished. That's what self-betrayal looks like.

Let's talk about what self-betrayal FEELS like. Self-betrayal is when you are doing something, and your inner voice is telling you not to do it and you do it anyway. All my life, ever since my conception, there has been a voice inside of me, some people call it intuition, some people call it a voice of reason. Whatever you call that voice, always remember, that voice inside of you will never lie to you. That voice inside of you has never lied to you. Although that voice has reminded you every time you were in a bad place, every time you wanted an answer to anything, that voice in you has always given you the answer. Sometimes you don't like the answer, but that voice has stayed with you and always guided you the right way. Even though you did not follow the instruction of that voice, that voice still never betrayed you because that voice is the presence of GOD.

After discovering that voice is GOD inside me, I realized that I betrayed GOD which was inevitably the biggest mistake I have ever made. I realized that the pain I felt was not from the narcissist but actually was from my betrayal of me and I am telling you that the pain you feel is the pain of self-betrayal. It is absolutely self-betrayal. You are not in pain because of what the narc did to you, you're in pain because of what You did to You.

The reason that you are still obsessively thinking of the narcissist, the reason why you cannot stop talking about the narcissist is because you are waiting for the narcissist to validate you for all the things you have done for them throughout the relationship, and the narcissist has not and will not validate your feelings.

<u>EXERCISE #3</u>: Make a list of all of the bad situations that you have experienced with the narcissist. Every time you ruminate, read that list as a reminder.

NOTES

____

____

____

____

____

____

____

____

____

____

____

CHAPTER 4

The Apology

You first have to acknowledge that you have done wrong. You must atone with yourself and know that your biggest mistake was the role you played in these events.

To heal the wounds that you created,

you owe yourself an **apology**.

<u>EXERCISE #4</u>: I want you to sit or stand in front of a mirror and as you see your reflection in the mirror, I want you to read the list of things that you tolerated from the narcissist and apologize to yourself for allowing yourself to tolerate all the bad on the list.

- I apologize for my betrayal.

- I apologize for betraying you.

- I apologize for being an active participant in my own demise.

- I apologize because I know better and knew better.

- I apologize because I am better.

- I apologize because I deserve forgiveness.

- I apologize because I am a good-hearted person.

- I apologize because I want my great relationship with me back.

- I apologize because it's my time to heal.

- I apologize for disrespecting myself and for demeaning myself.

- I apologize for engaging in arguments.

- I apologize for lowering my vibrations.

- I apologize for not listening to my inner voice.

- **I apologize because it's my turn to WIN!**

- **I apologize because I love ME!**

NOTES

____

____

____

____

____

____

____

CHAPTER 5

Forgiveness

So, you are blaming yourself for staying in a toxic relationship for so long, but there is a logical reason why you stayed in it. All throughout your life you have been groomed to stay in unhealthy relationships. You were told from a young age that relationships are hard and relationships are a lot of work. You were told that you need to stay in a relationship through thick and thin, even in the Bible, it states you should stay together for better and for worse.

After the apology you must stop blaming yourself and forgive yourself. After you acknowledge what you have done you will no longer feel guilty after admitting you did this to yourself, taking your power back after you acknowledge that you had control, not the narcissist. You have control over your vessel, not the narc.

The narcissists' greatest fear is not having control over you.

Acknowledge that after everything you went through, you had control over it and you have apologized, you have taken your power back from the narc because when you point the finger at the narc everything was their fault and you did nothing, you are also saying they have power over you. When you place the blame on the narcissist for your participation in an act that disrespects You, You are giving the narcissist power over You.

If you acknowledge that the narcissist does not have power over you, you had the power to not participate in the self-betrayal and chose not to use it, you are now taking your power back.

<u>EXERCISE #5</u>: Self-forgiveness is to first acknowledge that you did something wrong that you had control over. Its acknowledging that You had control, and you did not exercise your control and now you have apologized which will reset the way you think and the way you respond going forward. To forgive yourself means you will no longer hold your previous actions against yourself. It means that you won't say *"Damn, why I am so weak?"*; *"Why do I keep doing this to myself?"* Self-forgiveness is self-healing.

CHAPTER 6

Creating Boundaries

Now we are at the phase of boundaries. Let's define boundary, a boundary is a line that marks a limit of an area. You must create a boundary. A boundary that you will not break, no matter what. Make it a small boundary, a promise that you will uphold for the rest of your life. It is essential for everyone that lives a happy life to achieve happiness, you absolutely must have boundaries that you will not cross and that you will not allow others to cross.

Your boundary is like a personal cocoon, it is your safe space. A space that you protect with everything in you because it is the space that creates self-respect and dignity. It is your integrity. It is an announcement to the world that in order to have a relationship with me, you must respect my boundaries. Your boundary is your promise to You.

So, what is a **boundary**? A boundary is a mental wall that you have put in place so that no one can cross a line of that wall and still have a relationship with you that is happy or healthy and this includes yourself. You must have boundaries in place that you will not cross. This person never forced me physically, nor did she place a gun to my head to force me to deal with her. I completely voluntarily betrayed myself by participating in that situation from beginning to end. I realized it was not her, it was me. Just because the person started the argument, that doesn't mean that I had to participate and that's where I realized I lost. I had the power, the option, and the opportunity and I did not seize that moment to cut her off and end the abuse in the relationship. I did not take advantage of that opportunity and I betrayed myself again and again. If I would had cut her off before all of the self-betrayal, I would have felt empowered, I would have felt strong, and I would have confidence.

Arguing is a tool that a manipulator uses to destroy your boundaries. Accepting disrespect is a tool that destroys your boundaries because if you engage in an argument that is disrespectful then you have opened yourself for more and more disrespect and you also walked into a place where you are normalizing disrespect. A narcissist will not deal with someone who has boundaries. The only reason a narcissist deals with you is because you do not have any boundaries.

EXERCISE #6: Create a boundary that you will not cross. For example, I promise myself that I will not participate in any act that disrespects me, such as arguing with someone knowing this person's only intention is to disrespect me.

NOTES

____

____

____

____

____

____

____

____

____

____

____

CHAPTER 7

Self-Love

Now, the last action is **self-love**. The question is how do I love myself? How do I show myself love? The first thing that you are going to do is to define love! My definition of love is "UNCONDITIONAL SACRIFICE" and happiness. You have to determine what love means to you and what makes you happy in its truest form? What truly makes you happy, what naturally makes you feel good? *Is it the sunlight? Is it the moonlight? Is it the ocean? Is it fire?*

Think back to your childhood when you were happy and ask yourself what exactly was it that made you feel good? Remember that the answer to your happiness is what you felt in its simplest form. If being around family for Christmas brought you happiness and made you feel loved, break it down to its simplest form, you are the happiest when you're in a family gathering, you are happiest around family, that's what makes you happy.

Do you remember playing outside as a child, do you remember the good times, do you remember the things that made you feel good, and you thought this was how your life would be?

So now, I want you to flip the page but before you do, I want you to say these words when you turn the page and you see your reflection again, I want you to look at yourself directly in your eyes and I want you to say *I love you*. I want you to say *I love you, I thank you, I need you, you are my strength, you are my rock, you are my foundation, you are the one that is going to get me through this because this too shall pass. You are enough. I love you.* You are incredible. Remind the person in the mirror that You are your best friend. Thank you for being my best friend. It's my turn to win. Repeat this cycle every day.

<u>EXERCISE #7</u>: Close your eyes and imagine yourself in the park on a beautiful sunny day. You are sitting on a park bench looking into a field and you see yourself as a child playing. The child playing in the field sees you and approaches you. You start crying as the child approaches, and the child recognizes you and can see that you are him/her in the future. The child asks you, *why are you sad?* And now you must answer and say why you allowed yourself to go through all of this and tell your younger self how to avoid this from happening!

CHAPTER 8

The Breakthrough

So, you are still ruminating, You just want your mind back, you want your place of peace back, you want your place of happiness back, and you just can't seem to break through. Now you have to go super nova. Now you have to mentally override those ill feelings that you have of self- doubt, feelings of inadequacy, the fear that you did the wrong thing, the fear that the narc may not be who they showed you they are.

Now you must recalibrate the way you think by refusing to feel sad, you have to refuse to give that narc another day of your life, you have to refuse to continue to be unhappy. You must tell yourself I am happy, and I am going to be happy no matter what. You must say you refuse to be unhappy for another moment in your life. Your unhappiness stops now.

From now on, every day of my life will be a celebration of my accomplishments. Every day of my life will reflect my happiness, even the days that life is trying to put me down, those days are still beautiful happy days. I refuse to be unhappy. I refuse to be sad, my happiness and my life are under my control, under my will and my will... is that my life is happy every day. Every day. I have the power to be happy, I have the control to be happy, I have the right to be happy and it is my will to be happy... and I hold myself accountable to be happy every day.

I will stop making this personal, I am not special to the narcissist, and I did not receive any special treatment from the narcissist because everything that was done to me was done to everybody before me and will be done to everyone after me. The new person will be mistreated worse than I was.

EXERCISE #8: I want you to sit or stand in front of a mirror and as you see your reflection in the mirror, I want you to recite -"I have the power to be happy"; "I have the control to be happy"; "I have the right to be happy"; and "it is my will to be happy and I hold myself accountable to be happy every day" and every day I will choose my happiness. It is my turn to win.

CHAPTER 9

Closure

You must have closure in order to move forward. **Closure** means you have the answer that you've been searching for like, *"Why did you ruin the relationship?"; "Why did you destroy our family?"; "Why did you abuse me?"; "Why did you lie to me?"; "Why did you cheat?"*

Closure means you are not looking for the narc to come back nor are you going back, and you are not accepting the narc back. This is the final process of letting go. Your closure is the work you have already done. You did everything in your power to fix the relationship and every time you did the narc destroyed it. And if you put the relationship back together again, the narc will destroy it again.

In order for you to start feeling better you must now devalue the narcissist. When you find yourself searching for answers about your relationship ending, it means that the narcissist still has some level of value in your life. You still respect something about them.

You can NOT have any respect nor value for the narcissist. You must see the narcissist for who they really are. **The narcissists' greatest fear is not having control over you.** The narcissist is a Destroyer, not a builder. The narcissist does not have empathy. The narcissist is an empty vessel that will only torture empaths who don't know about them. The narcissist is here to let you down, to disappoint, to make you feel depressed, to make you feel less than, to create self- doubt... and no one will ever have peace with a narcissist.

You have escaped, you are the one who got away, and the narcissist will never get over you. You literally just beat the devil because his mission was to destroy you and He didn't. His job was to keep you from living in your purpose and He failed. Now, go live in your purpose; #WE WIN!

<u>EXERCISE #9:</u> You must devalue and lose any respect that you have for the narcissist by reading the list that you wrote of things the narcissist did while you were with them. Stop feeling sorry for the narcissist. You must value the narcissist the same way you value used toilet paper because the only thing you will ever have with a narcissist is hope.

Conclusion

I wrote this book to re-introduce You to yourself. This is not about the narcissist. This book is about You helping You and for the rest of your life, I want you to remember what happens when You betray You. That time of your life is over and now as you move forward hold yourself accountable, make everyone respect your boundaries and most of all always love You first. #WEWIN

NOTES

____

____

____

____

____

____

____

____

____

____

____

____

____

About the Author

Harry Thornton, better known as "HarioOvadtop", is a native of Washington, DC - Capitol Heights, Maryland. Mr. Thornton has been employed with the Federal Government for 28 years. Due to his personal experiences with past narcissistic relationships, he became the creator of his own YouTube Channel, "HarioOvadtop".

During his battle with bad relationships, there was a lack of resources to cope with this crippling disease, that led him to create his YouTube Channel in order to help provide therapy to anyone experiencing abuse in a relationship and to help guide individuals to identify narcissistic behavior via group sessions and one-on-one coaching.

Follow me on

FaceBook, Instagram, TikTok, Twitter, YouTube

Milton Keynes UK
Ingram Content Group UK Ltd.
UKHW020323220324
439789UK00007B/171